COMPOSER SHOWCASE
HAL LEONARD STUDENT PIANO LIBRARY

Desert e

SIX ORIGINAL PIANO SOLOS

BY CAROL KLOSE

CONTENTS

Editor: Margaret Otwell

ISBN-13: 978-1-4234-1142-0

HAL•LEONARD®
CORPORATION
7777 W. BLUEMOUND RD. P.O. BOX 13819 MILWAUKEE, WI 53213

In Australia Contact:
Hal Leonard Australia Pty. Ltd.
4 Lentara Court
Cheltenham, Victoria, 3192 Australia
Email: ausadmin@halleonard.com

Visit Hal Leonard Online at
www.halleonard.com

Introduction

Desert Suite is the counterpart to my previous book, *Coral Reef Suite*. Together, the collections represent my impressions of two exotic worlds far removed from the green farmlands and changing seasons of my home in Wisconsin.

The pieces in *Desert Suite* were inspired by vacations spent outside Wickenburg, Arizona, at the homes of my aunts, Margaret Wiltrakis, Lucile Kaslauskas, and Fran Kaslauskas, to whom I dedicate this book.

With my first visit years ago, I was drawn to the landscape, history, nature, and Native American culture of the Southwest desert. As I observed the endless scrubby foothills dotted with cactus and sagebrush, marveled at the ever-changing colors of distant mountain silhouettes, and absorbed the nature and history of the area, I felt compelled to put my impressions into music.

Like the images they portray, the pieces in *Desert Suite* are filled with contrast: soaring lyrical melodies interspersed with earthy motives in low open fifths; predictable rhythmic patterns juxtaposed with mixed meters; playful dance-like images offset by the dark colors of haunting spirits. Images in sound are supported by a combination of contemporary and traditional musical devices such as chromatic scales in contrary motion, open fifths, modal and atonal melodic and harmonic material, mixed meters, the use of the damper and *una corda* pedals, contrasting articulations and dynamics, "drum beats" created by tapping on the fallboard, and wide use of the extreme registers of the keyboard. Pedagogically, each piece focuses on technical skills that help express the image suggested by the title. These are listed in the Performance Notes.

I would like to thank Aunt Fran for sharing her love and knowledge of the desert, as she led our family on hikes through barren washes, Vulture Peak, the Hassayampa River bed, and hidden, dark canyons. It is to her memory that I dedicate the piece, "Desert In Bloom."

I hope that *Desert Suite* will inspire the performer to imagine, recreate, and savor the spirit and colors of the Southwest desert, a unique treasure of our most remarkable land.

—Carol Klose

Performance Notes

Dawn To Dusk

The changing moods in this piece reflect the progression of the desert day: from the quiet sunrise, through midday, to a meditation before the last rays of the setting sun. Pedagogical features include:
- Balance between the hands (melody and accompaniment).
- Smooth and graceful execution of slurred RH melodic lines.
- Careful observance of damper pedal markings, to achieve contrast between the lyrical main theme and the dry "earthy" open-fifth motive (as in measures 9-10).
- Observance of *ritardandos* and tempo changes in the transitions between large sections.

Gecko Games

In this piece, two playful geckos—one in the right hand and the other in the left—scamper in a game of chase among the rocks and stones on the desert floor. In the final measures, the two scurry away in opposite directions as fast as possible, with *presto* contrary-motion chromatic scales that die away to *ppp* as if hiding under a rock. Have fun!

The faster the piece is played, the less motion should be used, to facilitate the quick technical moves needed to bring the geckos to life. The performer should strive for:
- Short crisp *staccatos*, using a level but flexible wrist, and fingers that "pluck" the keys with a "hot potato" touch.
- *Vivace* tempo achieved by keeping the fingers close to the keys.
- Marked accents reinforced by arm weight and impulse playing.
- Careful attention to dynamics, especially in the last four measures, where the *una corda* pedal may be added to facilitate the rapid *decresc.* to the final *ppp*.

Desert In Bloom

This piece is an impression of the myriad exotic desert plants gently unfolding into a canvas of unexpected color after a rainfall. Grace-note figures in the introduction and *coda* imitate a bird song, while flowing eighth-note patterns in mixed meter in the body of the piece represent the blooms slowly emerging into sunlight. The RH 7/8 pattern in measure 9 is repeated on various pitches throughout, making the piece easy to learn.

One should be attentive to:
- Bringing out the LH *tenuto* notes, which form an underlying countermelody beneath the flowing RH patterns.
- Feeling the RH 7/8 rhythmic motive as "1-2-1-2-3-1-2," with a gentle pulse on each "1." The rhythm should flow effortlessly between meter changes, keeping eighth notes equal, whether in 3/4, 5/8 or 7/8 meter.
- Playing the arpeggiated chords with quiet ease from the bottom note to the top, as if setting the scene for the phrase that follows.

Canyon Spirits

Treading on the floor of a narrow, deep, dark canyon, one can almost feel the breath of desert spirits. The "half step, whole step, whole step" pattern is the basis for the eighth-note "spirit" motive. Eventually, the motive appears in rhythmic augmentation as LH half notes in measures 20-21. To achieve the eerie atonal sonorities, the RH eighth-notes should be as quiet as a whisper and blurred by the damper pedal, which is held down for several measures at a time, The *una corda* pedal should be depressed throughout.

Like spirits slowly rising from the canyon floor, the motives gradually rise to the high register of the piano. Their quiet, mysterious ascent is disturbed by sudden dissonant LH accents, with the earth below "calling out" in low open fifths. With the final chord deep in the bass, the spirits return to their home in the haunted canyon depths.

- For a mysterious, misty effect, keep the RH arm weight very steady, and depress the keys evenly, so as to produce as soft a tone as possible.
- Follow *cresc.* and *decresc.* markings carefully, to give the "spirits" movement.
- For half notes and whole notes with *staccato/tenuto* marks, use a slightly tapping touch, to allow the sound of each note to ring out.
- Observe the *rit.* and *a tempo* markings carefully, to "breathe" between groups of phrases.
- For the final chord, lean in closer to the keys, for a truly soft, ghostly sound.

Mother Earth, Sister Moon

Two contrasting ideas make up this piece, written in "Intro-ABA-*Coda*" form:
1. The strength of Mother Earth ("A"), characterized by a steady rhythmic pulse, the prevalence of fourths and well-articulated two-note slurs in the modal RH melody, supported by low open fifths in the accompaniment.

2. The shimmering ethereal quality of Sister Moon ("B"), with a flowing RH 16th-note melodic pattern in the high register, over a LH *arpeggio*-style accompaniment.

In the introduction and *coda*, the 16th-note "drum beats" may be played on the fallboard, either by tapping or knocking with the left hand. With the damper pedal down, the taps will set up sympathetic vibrations of their own, adding to the sonority. The drum beats may also be played by a second performer, using a percussion instrument, such as a tom-tom, rattle, or maracas. During the "Mother Earth" section, similar drum beat patterns may also be improvised by a second performer on percussion.

Kokopelli (Invention in Phrygian Mode)

One of the more familiar characters in Anasazi lore is Kokopelli, represented by a slightly bent-over figure playing a flute. Although there are varied versions of the legend, one suggests that Kokopelli was a trader who traveled throughout Mexico and the southwest, announcing his arrival in a village by playing his flute.

This sprightly dance-like piece is based on the E and A Phrygian modes (E F G A B C D E, and A B♭ C D E F G A). Two descending motives form the "subject" of the "invention:" a five-note pattern and a full Phrygian "scale" pattern. Loosely based on the style of a Bach Invention, the "subject" reappears in imitation and inversion throughout the piece. The LH chord in measure 1 is the harmonic basis for the episodic material, which follows in measures 5-7, 21-28, etc.

To perform this piece well,
- Play *staccatos* with a very short, crisp touch.
- Use a single impulse to execute all slurs, keeping the wrist flexible.
- Follow dynamic and pedal indications carefully, using them to build excitement throughout.
- Keep the momentum driving to the very last arpeggiated chord in measure 47, ending with strong fingers for the final statement *in tempo* at the end.

Dawn To Dusk

Carol Klose

5

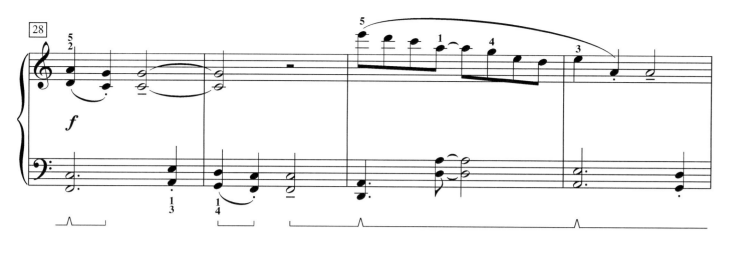

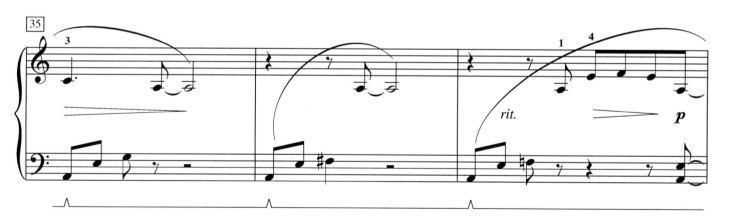

Slowly, with reverence ($\textbf{\textit{d}} = 58$)

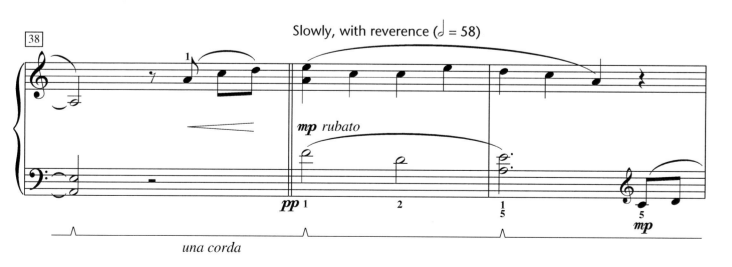

una corda

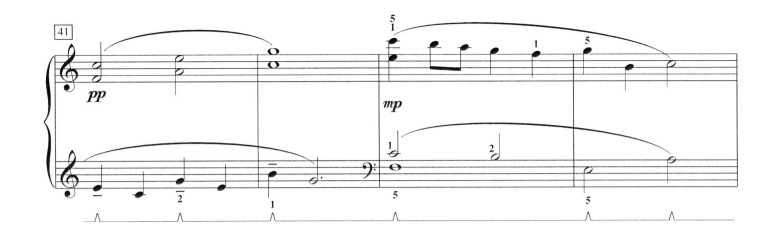

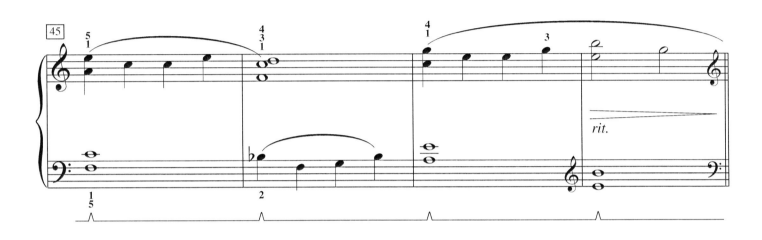

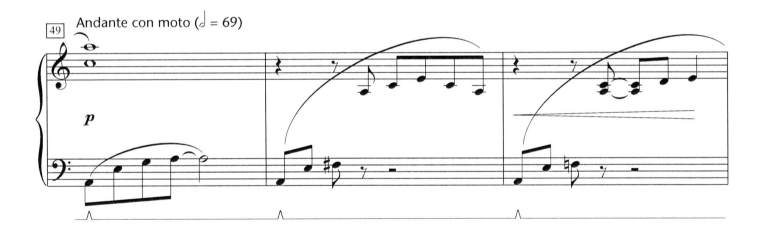

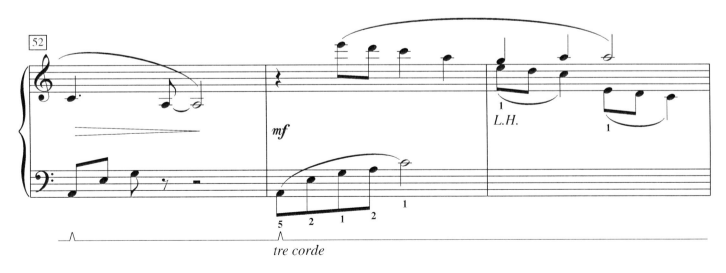

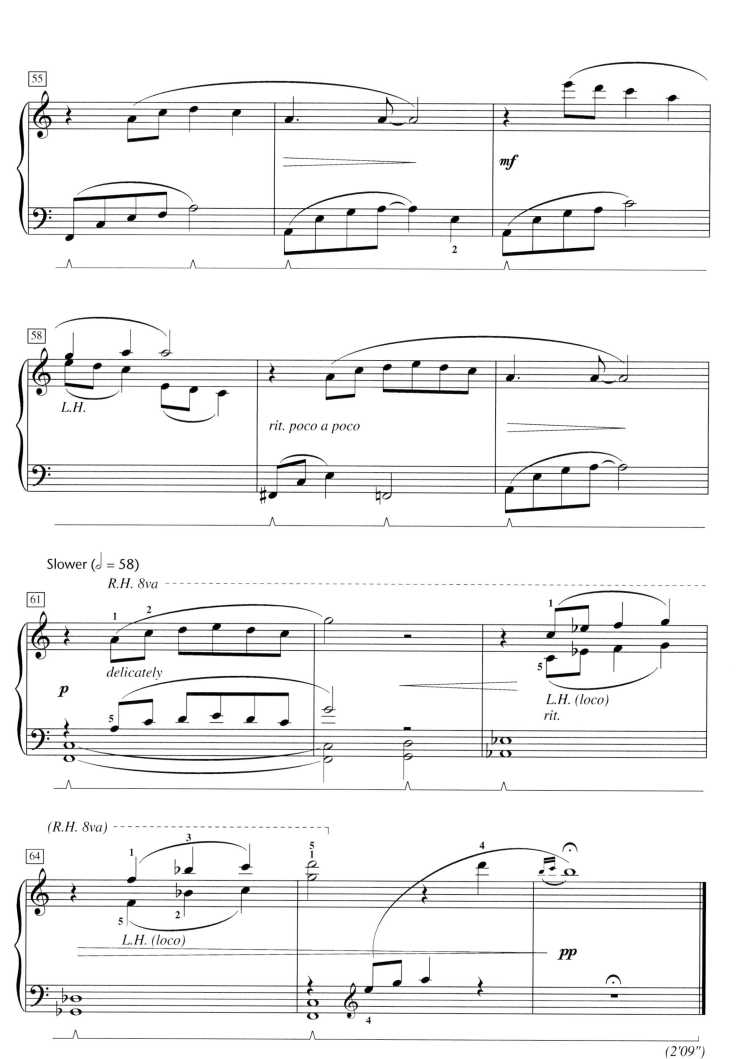

Slower (♩ = 58)

(2'09")

Gecko Games

Carol Klose

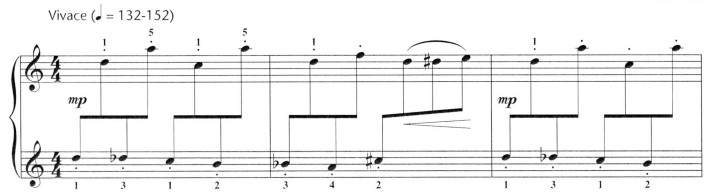

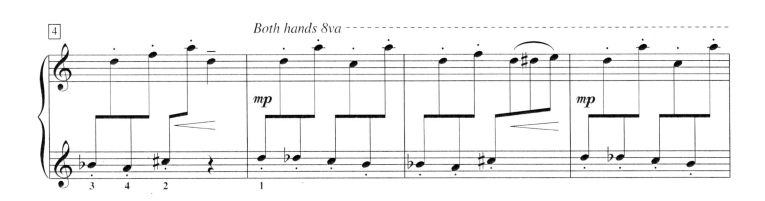

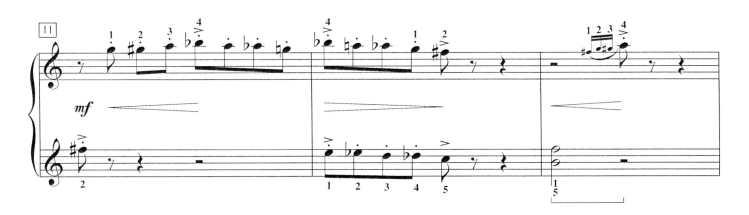

Desert In Bloom

For Aunt Fran

Carol Klose

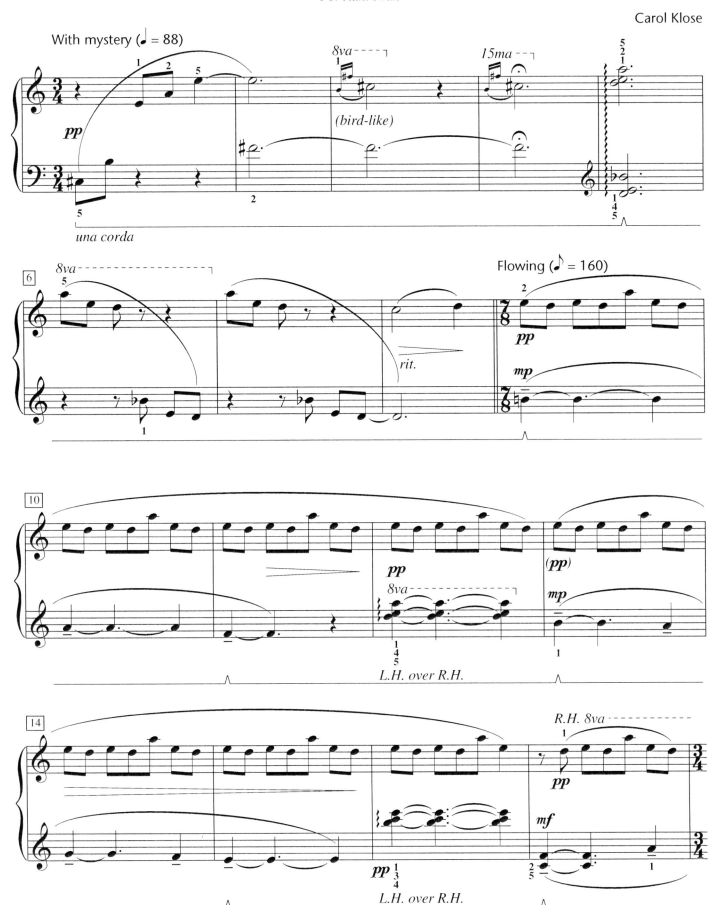

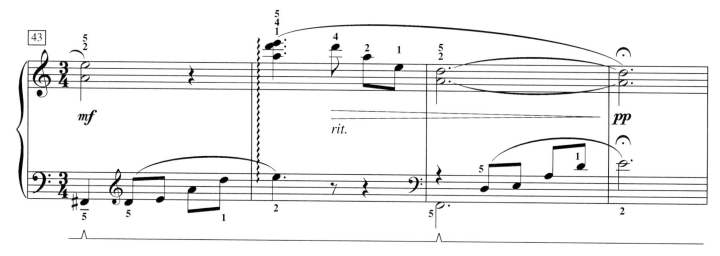

Canyon Spirits

Carol Klose

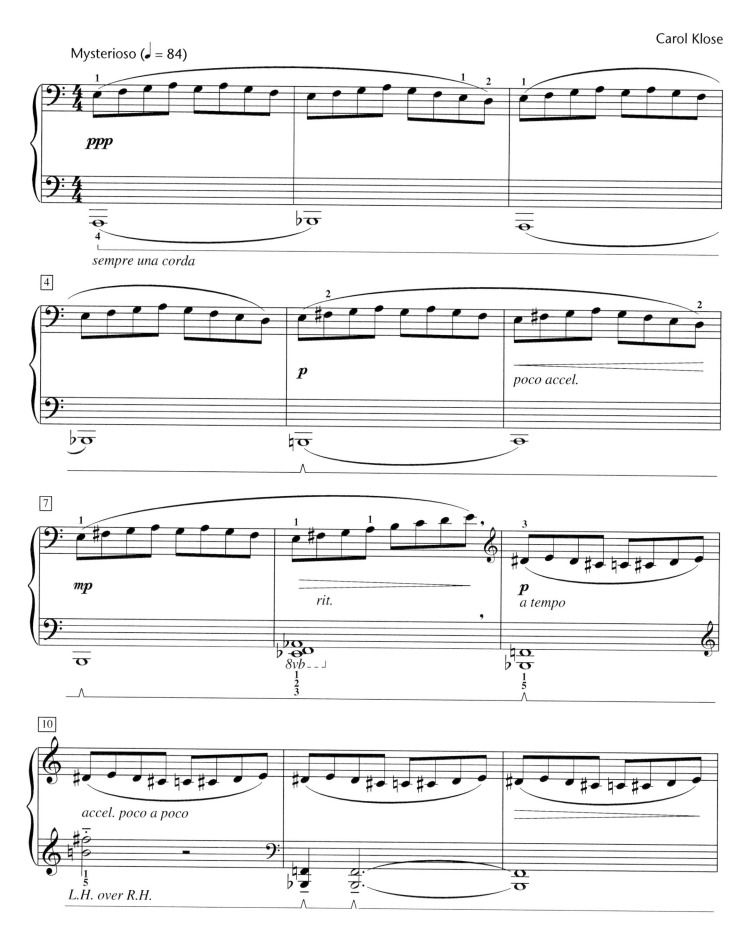

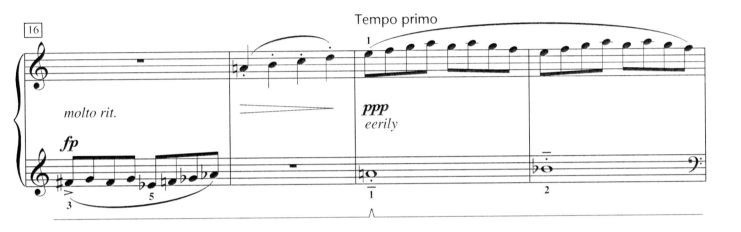

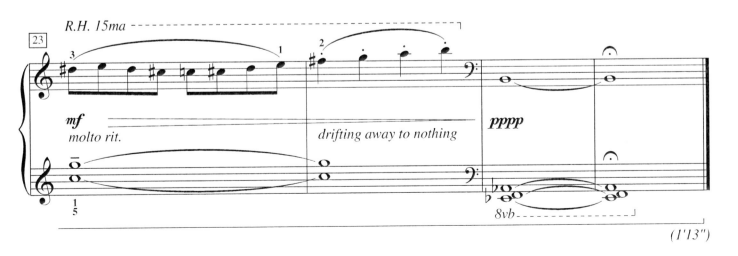

(1'13")

Mother Earth, Sister Moon

Carol Klose

18

"Sister Moon"

poco rit.

mp
a tempo

R.H. 8va -

cresc.

mf

mp

molto allarg.

f marcato
a tempo

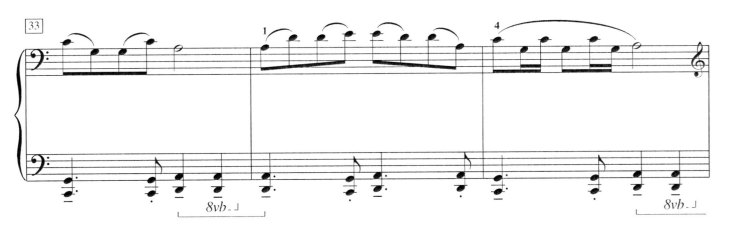

(2'27")

Kokopelli
(Invention In Phrygian Mode)

Carol Klose